Focus on the Philharmonic

Focus on the Philharmonic

In celebration of the 150th anniversary of the New York Philharmonic

Photographs and text by Bert Bial

Focus on the Philharmonic
text and photographs by Bert Bial

Library of Congress Catalog Card Number: 92-61176

Produced by Bob Adelman
Designed by Elton Robinson

Printed in Japan

Front cover: *Vladimir Tsypin   1985*

Title page: *Avram A. Lavin and Paul Clement   1988*

The distinct advantage Bert Bial has over most photographers in an orchestral situation is, of course, that he is a musician. Bert's knowledge of shutter-release coincides so meticulously with the music that sometimes, looking at his pictures of me conducting a certain work, I almost know exactly at which precise moment of music the photograph was taken. He is also extremely sensitive to his colleagues both onstage and backstage, and some of the photographs capture, especially on tour, moments of intimacy between musicians before going onstage. These are extremely revealing.

Because of Bert's long tenure with the New York Philharmonic, the wealth of pictures that has accumulated in his collection, I feel, must be shared with the rest of the world, and I, myself, cannot wait to distribute this book amongst my friends and to New York Philharmonic fans. I know that not only musicians but also the general public will derive immense pleasure from this book because all their favorite musicians, conductors and soloists have been captured in rare moments either on- or off-stage. I feel this work is long overdue.

ZUBIN MEHTA
March, 1991

The photographs in this book cover the period from 1957 to 1991. My position as contrabassoonist in the New York Philharmonic has given me an extraordinary vantage point from which to photograph orchestral musicians and some of the leading musical figures of our time. The intimacy gained from rehearsing, performing and traveling together so much forms, through the pictures, a kind of portrait of the New York Philharmonic.

These thirty-four years have been significant, especially the first ten years, because they represent an explosion of music making such as the world had never before seen. Leonard Bernstein, the long-playing record, jet travel, television, and particularly the year-round performance of symphonic concerts brought the New York Philharmonic to millions of people all over the globe. Not since the days of Arturo Toscanini and the Sunday afternoon radio broadcasts of the 1930's had a conductor and the New York Philharmonic been household words. Now it was Leonard Bernstein and the New York Philharmonic who had gained that familiarity and esteem.

Founded in 1842, the New York Philharmonic is the oldest orchestra in the United States and one of the oldest in the world. It performs more concerts per year than any other major orchestra and has one of the most extensive and varied repertoires. Not only does the orchestra perform with a tremendous number of conductors, but it has also followed the baton of composers such as Igor Stravinsky, Paul Hindemith and Aaron Copland, who have led the orchestra in interpretations of their own music. Some soloists have become conductors and an occasional orchestra member has also taken the podium…violists Leon Barzan and Larry Newland, for example, and trumpeter Gerard Schwartz.

Dimitri Mitropoulos 1958

My entry into this symphonic world took place at Lewisohn Stadium, uptown at 137th Street and St. Nicholas Avenue. The New York Philharmonic, during its six-week summer season, was at that time called the Stadium Concerts Orchestra. We played five rehearsals for five different programs each week. This repertoire was more than most orchestras played in a whole year! We had numerous guest conductors and soloists. The great variety of programs ranged from a night of all Gershwin to the singing of Dame Joan Sutherland to the conducting of Igor Stravinsky. In the fall, the New York Philharmonic's regular subscription season would begin at Carnegie Hall, at that time with Dimitri Mitropoulos on the podium.

Dimitri Mitropoulos

Mitropoulos' face, with eyes closed at times, had an almost mystical quality to it. His memory was legendary. At a rehearsal for a concert performance of Richard Strauss' *Elektra*, someone in the brass section asked if a certain sequence of notes in his part was correct. The details were somewhere buried in the middle of this vast orchestration. Mitropoulos, without referring to the huge opera score in front of him, closed his eyes for a few seconds and told the musician what the correct notation was. Not only had he memorized the music, but he had done so to the point that everything the composer had written was clearly visible to his remarkable mind.

Leonard Bernstein 1960's

I had had my apprenticeship with the Pittsburgh Symphony Orchestra under the direction of William Steinberg. (Years later he would have the honor of being named Principal Guest Conductor of the New York Philharmonic.) As disciplined as my experiences had been, nothing could have prepared me for the dramatic expressivity of a Mitropoulos. At one time, I actually stopped playing, almost hypnotized by him as he agonized over the death scene from Prokofiev's *Romeo and Juliet* Suite. I had to prod myself to resume playing.

Leonard Bernstein   Then came Lenny and off we flew into a new dimension. Lenny worked hard, very hard. And we worked hard, very, very hard. Playing with him wasn't always easy. In fact, he could be very difficult to follow. It could be wearying.

Once there were twelve weeks at Carnegie Hall during which we did not have a single day off. We were doing the normal subscription series with their usual rehearsals and overtime, plus extra concerts, TV shows, Young People's Concerts, and, of course, recordings. We were in a state of limbo, with a feeling of having moved into Carnegie Hall. Our work was stimulating. But towards the end of this twelve-week marathon, just seeing the Carnegie Hall façade, not to say entering the backstage area, became excruciating. We were thoroughly saturated.

Pierre Boulez 1970's

Then Lenny would go away for a while and we would settle back into a normal routine for a month, perhaps, with guest conductors. The normal routine meant four rehearsals for a program that is repeated four times each week, a relief from the never-ending, crushing hours.

In time, Lenny would return. With all our complaints, the truth was that performing with him meant a partnership in making unusually interesting and beautiful music. Isn't that what it's all about?

He gave us a lovely compliment once. In essence he said, "You're unbelievable. There's no orchestra in the world like you. If we perform Beethoven, you become a Beethoven orchestra; if we do Haydn, you sound like a Haydn orchestra; Webern, a Webern orchestra. You don't have a slick sound that sounds the same for everything."

Pierre Boulez   In 1971, Pierre Boulez became Music Director of the New York Philharmonic. Leonard Bernstein became Laureate Conductor. A comparison of their styles and approaches to the orchestra was an exercise in contrasts. The generous motions with which Lenny had led the orchestra gave way to the neat, precise gestures of Boulez. His was a very different and distinct probing of the orchestra and the music. Bernstein's manner was romantic and

Zubin Mehta 1980's

colorful; Boulez's authority came across as lean and concise. Some people felt Boulez distanced himself from the music, thereby creating a gulf between the audience and the music as well.

There was criticism for both from concertgoers. Some complained that Lenny's balletic conducting was distracting. Others grumbled that Boulez's explicit but sparse movements on the podium were unexpressive and monotonous to watch. Invariably, and with some impatience, I would say, "Why don't you close your eyes and just listen?" In their recordings with the New York Philharmonic, one can hear how each of these men, in his own distinctive way, made beautiful music.

Zubin Mehta In 1978, the New York Philharmonic again had a new conductor— Zubin Mehta. He was to become the longest-tenured Music Director in the orchestra's modern history. Once more, the musicians faced a sweeping shift in perspective and temperament. Zubin's clear, angular, thrusting motions governed his interpretations. His intense concentration, often coupled with scoreless readings, deeply and directly involved us with him. Eye met eye and sonorities blended into harmonies. He accompanied soloists with great sensitivity and an almost uncanny anticipation. It became a source of pleasure and pride that Zubin so often chose soloists from among the ranks of the New York Philharmonic to play in concerts at home and abroad. Zubin's tenure as Music Director is over, but the partnership we shared in performing so many concerts will long be remembered by us.

Concert   1970's   *Rehearsal, Zubin Mehta   1989*

In 1961 construction of Philharmonic Hall was still going on as we moved into our new home. The occasional nut or bolt that fell from above convinced Walter Botti and Robert Gladstone to don hard hats.

Hae-Young Ham, Gary Levinson in rehearsal 1990

Isadore Strassner 1959

Frederick Zimmerman 1961

In rehearsal at Royal Albert Hall with Murray Perahia and Zubin Mehta   1988

In rehearsal, 1970's, from left: Barry Lehr, Lorin Bernsohn, Raymond Sabinsky, Valentin Hirsu

Paul Neubauer, Glenn Dicterow, tour respite   1987

Alan Stepansky, Zubin Mehta   1989

Bernard Robbins   1980's

Randall Butler   1980's

Gerald Appleman, Allan Schiller, Henry Nigrine   1980's

Edward Erwin 1987

Walter Rosenberger, Elden Bailey   1960

Walter Rosenberger, Elden Bailey   1989

Elden Bailey, Christopher Lamb   1980's

From left: Joseph Robinson, Jeanne Baxtresser, Leonard Bernstein, Stanley Drucker, Judith LeClair   1986

Engelbert Brenner, Joseph Zizza   1961

Clockwise from left: Paige Brook, Stephen Freeman, Peter Simenauer, Michael Burgio, Stanley Drucker, Albert Goltzer, Julius Baker   1980's

Gilbert Cohen   1980's   Zubin Mehta, Sol Greitzer   1982

Nathan Milstein, Zubin Mehta 1980

Ranier De Intinis (foreground), Walter Rosenberger, Morris Lang   1980's

Lorin Bernsohn, Newton Mansfield   1980's   *Harold and Albert Goltzer   1970's*

Rehearsal break, Royal Albert Hall   1988

The need to practice is endless. We can always be seen onstage going over music, trimming reeds, even repeating scales. Actually, there is no one exact way to play anything and we all work hard for that elusive ideal of perfection. It is all so very serious. But we do have some lighter moments.

Years ago, a conductor by the name of Alfredo Antonini had a problem with a piece of music during rehearsal. He said, "Gentlemen, gentlemen, there's only one way to play this, and if that doesn't work, we'll do it another way."

Another quip went simply, "Who's sitting in that empty chair?"

So, chairs must not be empty. Problems are solved and the involvement with the music goes on.

Leonard Davis   1988

Martin Ormandy, brother of the late conductor Eugene Ormandy, is shown "secluded" in the percussion section, practicing. Lenny Davis sharpens his facility facing partitions. Matti Braun studies music on the librarians' table on tour. The constant confusion of sounds recedes in their concentration.

Matitiahu Braun   1987

Martin Ormandy   1959

Jerome Ashby, Schauspielhaus, East Berlin 1988

Eugene Becker, Teatro Juarez, Guanajuato, Mexico 1981

Philip Smith, Mindy Kaufman 1981

Carl Stern in a loge of Philharmonic Hall   1961   *Donald Harwood   1988*

Sarah Bullen   1988

Stanley Drucker   1980's

Peter Kenote   1987

William Vacchiano, Warsaw, Poland   1959

Oboist Harold Gomberg produced a huge, full, rich sound with such control and musicality that it was awesome. He was unique, weaving his creativity into the creations of others. Beethoven, Debussy or De Falla, all retained their temperaments within Gomberg's voice.

Oboist Harold Gomberg   1970's   *Philip Myers, Zubin Mehta   1980's*

From left: Carmine Fornarotto, Gerard Schwartz, James Smith, Edward Herman, Jr.,
Gilbert Cohen, Allen Ostrander   1970's

Librarians John Perkel and Lawrence Tarlow wait for Zubin Mehta to take the baton and begin the concert.   *1980's*

Zubin Mehta, Teatro Colon, Buenos Aires   1987

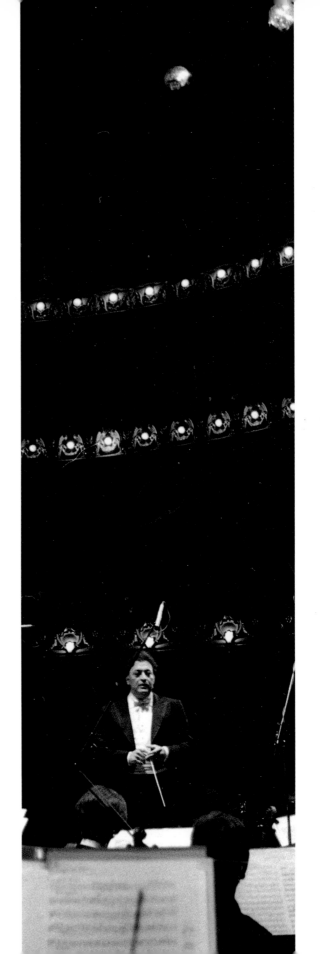

A television broadcast 1958

Pierre Boulez, Tokyo   1970's

On a very rare occasion, something other than the music can predominate. In other words, something goes wrong.

Years ago, in the early 1960's, Paul Paray was conducting Respighi's *Pines of Rome*. The score calls for what is now considered an old-fashioned phonograph recording of a nightingale chirping. The orchestral passages fade at this point and the soft melodious sounds of the nightingale are heard.

I am tacit in this movement and have the leisure to look about me. The phonograph "performer" was the late personnel manager, Joseph De Angelis. It was fascinating to watch the preparations for his "solo." He started and stopped the turntable several times, then took to experimenting with the tone arm. It seemed he was looking for a comfortable way to lower the needle quietly onto the record. First he held the tone arm by the head and practiced raising and lowering it a few times. Next he tried balancing it from the middle on a finger. That idea he gave up quickly. This was followed by manipulating and fingering the very rear of the tone arm where it pivoted.

At this point, De Angelis became aware that Paul Paray was animatedly gesturing at him. The nightingale was late in song. In a panic, De Angelis turned the knob that not only started the turntable but also fully boosted the volume. His right hand convulsively grabbed the tone arm and for a few seconds he seemed unable to release his grasp as he raked the phonograph needle back and forth on the record. The screeches heard on the over-amplified loudspeakers would have made even a large chorus of South American condors sound tame.

In his *New York Times* review of the concert the next day, Harold Schonberg entitled his column "Disaster Strikes the Nightingale at the Philharmonic."…Now a small tape deck is used.

Catastrophes like this do not abound. If we get one a decade, that is a lot.

Mindy Kaufman, Guanajuato, Mexico   1981

Nathan Milstein, Pierre Boulez   1976

Daniel Barenboim, Vladimir Ashkenazy 1971

Marc Ginsberg, Emanuel Ax   1990

Isaac Stern, Zubin Mehta, Concertgebouw, Amsterdam   1988

Erich Leinsdorf, Vladimir Spivakov, Bolshoi Hall, Leningrad   1976

Leonard Bernstein, Gregor Piatigorsky   1970

Zubin Mehta, Midori 1989

Jascha Heifetz, Hollywood Bowl 1963

Mstislav Rostropovich   1990

Rostropovich at a reception for the New York Philharmonic in Moscow   1959

Pinchas Zukerman, Charles Rex, Marc Ginsberg 1990

Zubin Mehta, Jessye Norman   1989   *Jennie Tourel   1964*

Luciano Pavarotti   1986   *Joan Sutherland   1960's*

Rudolf Serkin 1960

Rudolph Serkin was in the old Green Room in Carnegie Hall, waiting to rehearse. Yes, I could take pictures, but please no flash. He wanted to concentrate on the Beethoven concerto. Agitated, he paced back and forth wringing his hands and humming to himself. I felt a terrible tension in the room and I tried to disappear by wedging myself into a corner between the studio piano and the wall. He'd pause, peer out the window somewhat sightlessly it seemed, and again hum bits of the Beethoven.

I quickly took six pictures and fled.

Robert Casadesus 1961

Cellist Natalia Gutman with Eugene Levinson, Emanuel Boder, Mark Schmoockler, Bernardo Altmann 1989

Eileen Farrell 1976

Itzhak Perlman, Zubin Mehta   1989

Glenn Gould   1960's

Glenn Gould was staying at the Carlyle Hotel on Madison Avenue when I came to show him the photos I had taken of him a few months earlier. Pulling his hand back quickly when I extended mine for a handshake, he smiled and informed me that he never shook hands with anyone, but please come in.

His friendly manner was appealing. Did he remember me standing next to him, months ago, just offstage when he was fuming with anger? His fury was directed at Lenny because Lenny was at that moment addressing the Carnegie Hall audience about what they were about to hear. Lenny was informing them that Glenn Gould had his very own individualistic ideas about how to play the Brahms Piano Concerto, how slow it had to be, and that rapport between them was absent.

In backstage counterpoint, Gould was muttering that Lenny didn't have to justify his presence on the stage. If he didn't like Gould's interpretation, why didn't Lenny let the assistant conductor take over? Why didn't he let the audience decide for themselves if they liked the performance? Who needed anyone's opinion? Or maybe he (Gould) just wouldn't perform.

It was fascinating. As a matter of fact, our music stands did hold a substitute Brahms symphony, just in case Gould refused to play. He did play.

Van Cliburn, John Corigliano in background 1958

Artur Rubinstein   1975

Isaac Stern, Carnegie Hall   1960's

Joseph Szigeti   1959

Igor Stravinsky, Lewisohn Stadium   1960's

One day, I decided that Igor Stravinsky might appreciate a photo I had taken of him conducting us. I would make him a gift of it and perhaps it would help me overcome a tongue-tied awe that sometimes plagued me. Maybe we could even have a chat. It didn't work out quite that way.

I approached Stravinsky in his dressing room at Lewisohn Stadium. Stravinsky's amanuensis Robert Craft was there too. I presented Stravinsky with the photograph and I said something about my strong admiration for his music. He smiled and asked for a pen to sign the picture. No, I said, the picture was for him. He seemed very pleased but, again, and this time making writing gestures, he said to Craft that he needed a pen. It had never occurred to me that Stravinsky had lost some of his hearing. At this point, Craft started to scream at him, "Meister, he's giving you a gift. He doesn't want your autograph. He's giving you the picture."

Stravinsky beamed and did say "Thank you." I may even have said "Thank you" too. Who knows now.

Paul Hindemith's appearance with us months later prompted me to try again. This time things worked out a little differently, but it ended this kind of approach to the masters on my part.

Hindemith was waiting for an elevator in what was then the new Philharmonic Hall. I was just on my way upstairs to look for him and there he was. I said simply that I enjoyed his music and as a way of saying "Thank you," here was a picture of him conducting us the day before. He seemed terribly embarrassed and uncomfortable. Perhaps he misunderstood. Perhaps he thought I would hound him until he gave me, at the very least, the autographed original score of *Mathis der Maler* by way of payment. I quickly repeated, "Mr. Hindemith, it's a gift for you." He turned his head and quickly disappeared behind the closing elevator doors.

These two experiences stand alone but they did alter my "bearing of gifts."

Paul Hindemith 1963

Aaron Copland 1971

*The long wand on the contraption behind Leonard Bernstein made a
complete revolution in one minute. John Cage is explaining how to fit our
"notes" or "constellation" (Cage's term) to the cycle of this baton. To the
right of Cage are John Corigliano and Frank Gullino   1964*

John Cage   1980's

Two conductors for one piece: composer Earle Brown and Leonard Bernstein   1964

Lukas Foss   1959

William Schuman   1980's

Zubin Mehta, Oliver Knussen   1984

William Steinberg 1968

Thomas Schippers, Bolshoi Hall, Leningrad 1976

Gennady Rozhdestvensky, Glenn Dicterow at right   1988

Pierre Monteux   1959

Rafael Kubelik, Rodney Friend at right 1976

Bruno Walter   1960

Sarah Caldwell 1975

Yehudi Menuhin, Oscar Weizner 1971

Sir John Barbirolli, John Corigliano   1959

Leopold Stokowski   1968

A gathering of composers   Top row: *David Del Tredici, Earl Brown, Steve Reich, Stanley Silverman, John Cage, Elliott Carter*

Second row: *Donald Martino, Donald Harris, unidentified, Morton Gould, Vincent Persichetti, Roy Harris*

Third row: Assistant Conductor David Gilbert, Stephen Jablonski, Jacob Druckman, Roger Sessions, William Schuman, Aaron Copland

Front row: Milton Babbitt, Lucia Dlugoszewski, Ulysses Kay, George Rochberg. Pierre Boulez at right   1976

Erich Leinsdorf   1989   *Leonard Slatkin (center) with composers Donald Erb (left) and Jacob Druckman*

Aaron Copland, Leonard Bernstein, Philharmonic Hall   1962

George Walker at New York Philharmonic rehearsal of his music at Juilliard   1980's

Nadia Boulanger, Carnegie Hall   1962

Leonard Bernstein, Dmitri Shostakovich, Bolshoi Hall, Moscow   1959

Leonard Bernstein, violinist Jack Benny   1959

Carl Sandburg, Andre Kostelanetz   1963

Peter Ustinov, Young People's Concert rehearsal   1970

Diane Keaton, Woody Allen and Zubin Mehta at rehearsal of soundtrack for film, Manhattan   1978

Danny Kaye, Glenn Dicterow 1981

Dmitri Shostakovich 1959

From left: Felicia and Leonard Bernstein, Boris Pasternak, David M.
Kaiser (President of New York Philharmonic) and Sol Hurok, Moscow 1959

Prince Rainier III, Princess Grace with Nathan Goldstein and Frank Ruggieri, Monaco   1968

From left: Walter Rosenberger and Gerry Mulligan, chance meeting, Milan   1980's

Leonard Bernstein, James Levine, "Music for Life," Carnegie Hall   1987

Leonard Bernstein, Michael Jackson, Royce Hall, UCLA   1986

Assistant Manager William Weissel, Leonard Bernstein   1970's

Leonard Bernstein, football, Australia   1974

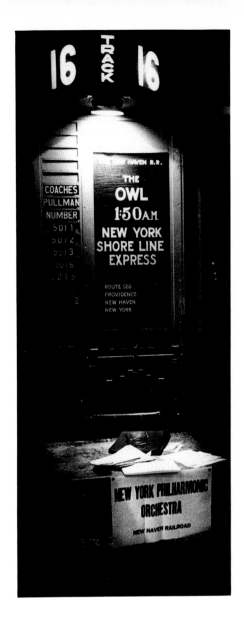

Omaha   1983

1960's

Rehearsing under sun screen, Hollywood Bowl   1983

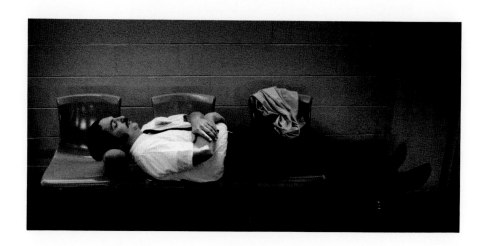

Clockwise from right: Marc Ginsberg, Evangeline Benedetti, Hanna Lachert, Mindy Kaufman, Sherry Sylar, Marina Kruglikov, Hoechst 1975

Gerald Appleman, airport 1980

Tour trunks, Turku, Finland 1959

Sale of folk instrument to Joseph and Mary Kay Robinson and their children, Istanbul 1985

Seiji Ozawa (2nd left) and Leonard Bernstein (4th left) at a New York Philharmonic Penguins softball game in Japan 1970

Bombay, India   1984

Evangeline Benedetti and python, Bangkok   1984

William Blossom, Bangkok 1989

From left: James Candido, Nathan Stutch, L. William Kuyper, Bernice Rosenberger, Istanbul 1985

William Bell, Seymour Lipkin, Dimitry Markevitch in foreground, Moscow 1959

Stagehand Louis Patalano and Zubin Mehta, Pre-rehearsal, Herodes Atticus, Athens   1985

Leonard Bernstein, Herodes Atticus Theatre, Athens   1959   *Outdoor concert, Baalbek, Lebanon*   1959

Leningrad   1976

Dresden, intermission   1985

Backstage, Warsaw   *1959*

At a party in Moscow in 1959, our hosts entertained the New York Philharmonic with many of their leading musicians. Unfortunately, they had not communicated the idea that we were to reciprocate. Some impromptu chamber music was hurriedly prepared, but Lenny had jazz on his mind. His collaborators were Philharmonic musicians Morris (Arnie) Lang on drums and Robert Gladstone on bass. If I recall correctly, the Russians were somewhat shocked. Nonetheless, we all had a good time. It was one of those thaws in the cold war.

Personnel Manager Carl Schiebler calls for silence and tuning. Rehearsal for free concert. Ibirapuera Park, São Paulo   1987

New York City   1958

Carlos Moseley, Associate Managing Director   1959

Managerial conference, from left: Albert K. Webster, William Weissel, Frank Milburn   1960's

From left: David M. Kaiser, President of New York Philharmonic, George Judd, Jr., Managing Director,
Joseph DeAngelis, Personnel Manager, Lewisohn Stadium   1959

Personnel Manager James Chambers, Leonard Bernstein, Ravinia   1986

Leonard Bernstein, Managing Director Bruno Zirato   1958

Managing Director Deborah Borda, Central Park, NYC   1991

General Manager Allison Vulgamore   1991

The New York Philharmonic entered a new epoch in 1991 with
the appointment of Kurt Masur as Music Director. The
audiences have shown a warmth and excitement about our
performances and look to Kurt Masur to establish his own legacy
with this venerable orchestra.

Kurt Masur   1991

NEW YORK PHILHARMONIC (1957)

Principal Conductors: Dimitri Mitropoulos, Leonard Bernstein
Guest Conductors: Ernest Ansermet, André Cluytens, Aaron Copland,
André Kostelanetz, Rafael Kubelik, Fernando Previtali,
Thomas Schippers, Robert Shaw
Associate Conductor: Franco Autori
Musical Director, Young People's Concerts: Leonard Bernstein

VIOLINS
John Corigliano
Concertmaster

Michael Rosenker
Asst. Concertmaster

Frank Gullino
David Rosensweig
Joseph Bernstein
Michael de Stefano
William Dembinsky
George Rabin
William Nowinski
Louis Fishzohn
Joachim Fishberg
Leon Temerson
Leon Rudin
Leopold Busch
Max Weiner
Morris Borodkin
Bjoern Andreasson
Mordecai Dayan

Leopold Rybb
Arthur Schuller
Armand Neveux
Imre Pogany
Bernard Robbins
Alfio Micci
Louis Carlini
Socrate Barozzi
Carlos Piantini
Carlo Renzulli
Isidor Strassner
Martin Eshelman
Morris Kreiselman
Louis Sherman
Robert de Pasquale
Alfred Lora

VIOLAS
William Lincer
Leonard Davis
David Kates
Sol Greitzer
Joseph Vieland
Elias Lifschey
Ralph Mendelsohn
Selig Posner
Eugene Becker
Robert Weinrebe
Henry Nigrine
Raymond Sabinsky

CELLOS
Laszlo Varga
Carl Stern
Naoum Dinger
Rudolph Sims
Nathan Stutch
Martin Ormandy
Mario Caiati
Milton Forstat
Heinrich Joachim
George Feher
Bernard Altmann
Asher Richman

BASSES
Robert Brennand
Frederick Zimmermann
Carlo Raviola
John Schaeffer
William Chartoff
Mario Polisi
Benjamin Schlossberg
Walter Botti
Robert Gladstone

FLUTES
John Wummer
Robert Morris
Paige Brook

PICCOLO
F. William Heim

OBOES
Harold Gomberg
Engelbert Brenner
Albert Goltzer

ENGLISH HORN
Michel Nazzi

CLARINETS
Robert McGinnis
Napoleon Cerminara

E-FLAT CLARINET
Stanley Drucker

BASS CLARINET
Leonard Schaller

BASSOONS
William Polisi
Frank Ruggieri
Manuel Zegler

CONTRABASSOON
Bert Bial

HORNS
James Chambers
Joseph Singer
Louis Ricci
Ranier De Intinis
Marcus Fischer
William Namen

TRUMPETS
William Vacchiano
Nathan Prager
John Ware
James Smith

TROMBONES
Edward Herman, Jr.
Lewis Van Haney
Allen Ostrander

TUBA
William Bell

TIMPANI
Saul Goodman

PERCUSSION
Walter Rosenberger
Elden Bailey
Morris Lang

HARP
Christine Stavrache

PIANO, ORGAN, HARPSICHORD
Bruce Prince-Joseph

ORCHESTRAL PERSONNEL MANAGER
Joseph De Angelis

ASSISTANT PERSONNEL MANAGER
Armand Neveux

PRESS DIRECTOR
Carlos Moseley

LIBRARIAN
Howard Keresey

ASSISTANT LIBRARIAN
Joseph Zizza

STAGE PERSONNEL
Francis Nelson
Peter Regan

NEW YORK PHILHARMONIC (1992)

Kurt Masur, *Music Director*
Samuel Wong, *Assistant Conductor*
Leonard Bernstein, *Laureate Conductor, 1943–1990*

VIOLINS
Glenn Dicterow
Concertmaster
The Charles E. Culpeper
Chair
Charles Rex
Associate Concertmaster
The William Petschek
Family Chair
Kenneth Gordon
Assistant Concertmaster
Enrico Di Cecco
Carol Webb
Yoko Takebe

Gabriel Banat
Emanuel Boder
Gary Levinson
Newton Mansfield
Kerry McDermott
Gino Sambuco
Allan Schiller
Fiona Simon
Richard Simon
Max Weiner
Oscar Weizner
Donald Whyte

Marc Ginsberg
Principal
Vladimir Tsypin
Assistant Principal
Jacques Margolies
Oscar Ravina

Matitiahu Braun
Marilyn Dubow
Martin Eshelman
Michael Gilbert
Judith Ginsberg
Nathan Goldstein
Hae-Young Ham
Myung-Hi Kim
Hanna Lachert
Daniel Reed
Mark Schmoockler
Sharon Yamada

VIOLAS
Irene Breslaw
Acting Principal
Rebecca Young
Associate Principal
Dorian Rence
Acting Assistant Principal
Katherine Greene

Peter Kenote
Barry Lehr
Kenneth Mirkin
Judith Nelson
Dawn Riggs
Mary Helen Ewing
Replacement
Mary Bishop Gigliotti
Replacement

CELLOS
Lorne Munroe
Principal
The Fan Fox and Leslie R.
Samuels Chair
Alan Stepansky
Associate Principal
Gerald K. Appleman
Assistant Principal
Evangeline Benedetti

Bernardo Altmann
Lorin Bernsohn
Paul Clement
Nancy Donaruma
Valentin Hirsu
Avram A. Lavin
Thomas Liberti
Asher Richman
On Leave
Avron Coleman
Replacement

BASSES
Eugene Levinson
Principal
The Redfield D. Beckwith
Chair
Jon Deak
Associate Principal
Orin O'Brien
James V. Candido

William Blossom
Walter Botti
Randall Butler
Lew Norton
Michele Saxon
John Schaeffer

FLUTES
Jeanne Baxtresser
Principal
The Lila Acheson Wallace
Chair
Sandra Church
Associate Principal
Renée Siebert
Mindy Kaufman

PICCOLO
Mindy Kaufman

OBOES
Joseph Robinson
Principal
The Alice Tully Chair
Sherry Sylar
Associate Principal
Jerome Roth

ENGLISH HORN
Thomas Stacy

CLARINETS
Stanley Drucker
Principal
The Edna and
W. Van Alan Clark Chair
Peter Simenauer
Associate Principal
Michael Burgio
Stephen Freeman

E-FLAT CLARINET
Peter Simenauer

BASS CLARINET
Stephen Freeman

BASSOONS
Judith LeClair
Principal
The Pels Family Chair
David Carroll
Associate Principal
Leonard Hindell
Bert Bial

CONTRABASSOON
Bert Bial

HORNS
Philip Myers
Principal
The Ruth F. and
Alan J. Broder Chair
Jerome Ashby
Associate Principal
L. William Kuyper
Assistant Principal
John Carabella
Ranier De Intinis
Aubrey Facenda

TRUMPETS
Philip Smith
Principal
George F. Coble
Associate Principal
Vincent Penzarella
Carmine Fornarotto

TROMBONES
Joseph Alessi
Principal
David Finlayson
Edward Erwin
Assistant Principal

BASS TROMBONE
Donald Harwood

TUBA
Warren Deck
Principal

TIMPANI
Roland Kohloff
Principal
The Carlos Moseley Chair
Morris Lang
Associate Principal

PERCUSSION
Christopher S. Lamb
Principal
The Constance R. Hoguet
Friends of the Philharmonic Chair
Morris Lang
Daniel Druckman

HARP
Sarah Bullen
Principal
Ruth Negri

KEYBOARD
In Memory of Paul Jacobs
HARPSICHORD
Lionel Party
ORGAN
Leonard Raver
PIANO
Harriet Wingreen
Jonathan Feldman

ORCHESTRA PERSONNEL
MANAGER
Carl R. Schiebler

ASSISTANT ORCHESTRA
PERSONNEL MANAGER
John Schaeffer

LIBRARIANS
Lawrence Tarlow
Principal
John Perkel
Assistant Principal
Thad Marciniak

STAGE REPRESENTATIVE
Louis J. Patalano

The New York Philharmonic has enriched our lives. In performing with this great orchestra, we have experienced a unique reality borne on configured sound.

Bert Bial, Sydney Harbour, Australia   1974